English

10 Minute Tests

10–11+ years

TEST 1: **Mixed**

Test time: 0 5 10 minutes

Rewrite these sentences changing them from plural to singular.

1 The leaves fell from the trees.

____

2 The children played with two skipping ropes and some footballs.

____

3 While playing, the kittens knocked the bags to the floor.

____

4 The swings broke and injured many children.

____

Change each of the nouns in bold to the *infinitive* of the verb.

5 Amil needed more practice with his **division**. to ____________

6 A **statement** was read out by the lawyer. to ____________

7 The **infection** had spread to Ella's ears. to ____________

8 The burglar was caught by the **detective**. to ____________

Write an *antonym* for each of these words by adding a prefix.

9	happy	____________	12	correct	____________
10	frost	____________	13	clean	____________
11	grateful	____________	14	advantage	____________

Complete the following proverbs.

15 Too many cooks ______________________________.

16 The grass is always greener ______________________________.

17 ______________________________ the mice will play.

18 ______________________________ has a silver lining.

19 The early bird ______________________________.

Write 'there', 'their' or 'they're' in the gap.

20 The children collected __________ bags before going home.

21–22 James and Sarah love __________ dog and __________ always taking him on long walks.

23 __________ is never enough money collected to help look after the homeless.

Complete these word sums. Watch out for the spelling changes!

24 busy + ly = __________

25 argue + ment = __________

26 laugh + ing = __________

27 notice + able = __________

28 complete + ly = __________

29 imagine + ary = __________

30 meaning + less = __________

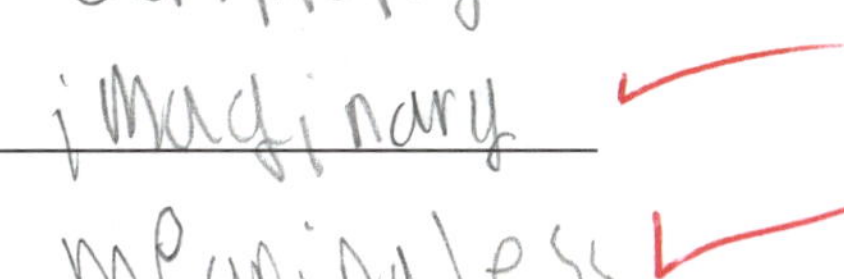

Total ______ / 30

TEST 2: Spelling

Test time: 0 5 10 minutes

Write each of these words correctly.

1 unecessary ____________________

2 desparate ____________________

3 recomend ____________________

4 apreciate ____________________

5 haras ____________________

6 detemined ____________________

7 bargin ____________________

8 enviroment ____________________

9 interupt ____________________

10 curiocity ____________________

Add a prefix to each of these to make a new word.

11 behave ____________________

12 charge ____________________

13 cycle ____________________

14 mobile ____________________

15 ready ____________________

16 fortune ____________________

Write four words, two ending in *cial* and two ending in *tial*.

17–18 ____________________ ____________________

19–20 ____________________ ____________________

Write the plural forms of these words.

21 church ______________

22 waltz ______________

23 bush ______________

24 pencil ______________

25 wife ______________

Add ie or ei to each of these to make a word.

26 br ___ ___ f

27 sl ___ ___ gh

28 ___ ___ ghty

29 f ___ ___ rce

30 f ___ ___ nt

31 s ___ ___ ge

32 r ___ ___ gn

33 c ___ ___ ling

Each of these words has a missing silent letter. Rewrite each word correctly.

34 nockout ______________

35 colum ______________

36 miniture ______________

37 salm ______________

38 nat ______________

39 climer ______________

40 nome ______________

Total

Test 3: Comprehension

Test time: 0 5 10 minutes

Read this extract carefully.

Nat and the Great Bath Climb *by Penelope Lively*

Wood-lice colonies are governed by Chief Wood-lice, who are stern and ancient creatures with whiskers of immense length. Young wood-lice are kept under the most strict control by their elders; indeed they are quite literally trampled on until large enough to hold their own. Wood-lice are not creatures who go in much for expressing themselves or being original or striking out; one wood-louse acts and thinks much like another and this is the way the old wood-lice want to keep it.

From time to time the Chief Wood-louse would call the whole colony together for a meeting. The object of this meeting was for the Chief Wood-louse to lecture the newest generation of young wood-lice, who were allowed to attend as soon as their whiskers were three millimetres long, which meant they were grown-up.

The hero of this story, who was called Nat, came to his first such meeting when he was three weeks old – which in human terms is about eighteen years. The young wood-lice sat in a row at the front, feeling important but nervous, while their parents and aunts and uncles crowded behind them and the Chief Wood-louse took up a position in front.

The Chief Wood-louse looked sternly down at the **assembled** crowd and began to speak. "We are gathered together today," he said, "to remind ourselves of the purpose of life." He glared at the young wood-lice. "And what is the purpose of life?" The young wood-lice, who knew they were not supposed to answer, gazed at him respectfully.

"The purpose of life is to climb up the side of the bath. That is what we are here for. That is why we were born. No one has ever succeeded. But the purpose of life is to try. Each and every one of us. Your turn has now come. Your mothers and fathers have tried before you. Some brave spirits have tried several times. All have failed."

There was silence. The young wood-lice gazed at the Chief Wood-louse and felt even more nervous and important. All except Nat, who was the youngest and smallest and had been in trouble most of his life for asking too many questions. Nat was thinking.

"You will make your attempts turn and turn about, starting with the eldest. Each of you will fail, but will have made a glorious attempt, you will then have your names inscribed on the Roll of Honour."

The young wood-lice went quite pink with pride and excitement, all except Nat, who raised one of his fourteen legs. "Please, sir," he said, "why do we have to climb up the side of the bath?"

There was a gasp of horror from the crowd of wood-lice. Nat's mother fainted clean away; his father bent his head in shame.

The Chief Wood-louse stared at Nat. His whiskers twitched in fury. "WHAT DID YOU SAY?"

Nat cleared his throat and repeated, politely and clearly, "Why do we have to climb up the side of the bath?"

The Chief Wood-louse huffed and puffed; his little black eyes bulged; **he creaked with indignation**. "BECAUSE IT'S THERE!" he roared…

Answer these questions about the extract.

1 Who controls young wood-lice?

2 Write a sentence describing what wood-lice elders are like.

3 How long do wood-lice whiskers have to be before wood-lice are considered to be grown-up?

4 How do you think the parents of the young wood-lice felt, waiting for the Chief Wood-louse to begin the meeting?

5 What is the meeting for?

6 Why had Nat been in trouble for most of his life?

7 What does the word **'assembled'** mean?

8 What is meant by **'he creaked with indignation'**?

9 Why were all the wood-lice shocked when Nat asked a question?

10 What do you think happened next?

Total

Test 4: Mixed

Test time: 0 5 10 minutes

Add to each of these words to make a compound word.

1 sun ______ sunbeam

2 hand ______ handrest

3 snow ______ snowstorm

4 pen ______ penpull

5 light ______

6 trap ______ traped

7 foot ______ footrest

8 rain ______ raindrop

Change these sentences into *reported speech*.

9 "If we don't hurry we'll be late," shouted Zoe.

Zoe told them to hurry up or they would be late.

10 Beth enquired, "Is this the way to the toilets?"

Beth asked were the toilets were.

11 "Quick, the guard dog is catching us!" screamed Dan.

Dan told them to be quick because the guard dog was catching them.

12 "What time is it?" asked Mrs Sparks.

Mrs Sparks asked whate time it was.

13 Mum whispered, "Remember, when you wake up in the morning it will be your birthday!"

______

______

Write a *homophone* for each of these words.

14 cereal ceriel

15 great grate

16 horse ______________

17 bough ______________

18 beach ______________

19 heard herd

20 wait wate

21 piece pee

22 sent cent

Punctuate this passage correctly. Remember to start a new line when it is needed.

23–40 Class 6 was having a swimming lesson I'm exhausted exclaimed Eva I wish something more exciting would happen I agree because if I do one more length of this pool I'll scream moaned Lee Suddenly Eva's wish came true as Mrs Davey their teacher slipped on some water at the side of the pool She fell headfirst into the pool

Class 6 was having a swimming lesson. "I'm exhausted," exclaimed Eva, "I wish something more exiting would happen!" "I agree because if I do one more lap I'll scream" Moaned Lee. Suddenly Eva's wish came true. As Mrs Davey their teacher slipped on some water at the side of the pool. She fell head first into the pool.

Time for a break! Go to Puzzle Page 42

Total

Test 5: **Vocabulary**

Test time: 0 5 10 minutes

Write an informal equivalent for each of these words.

1 request ____________________

2 displeasure ____________________

3 unavoidable ____________________

4 discover ____________________

5 **enter** ____________________

Write six *synonyms* for the word 'said'.

6 ____________________

7 ____________________

8 ____________________

9 ____________________

10 ____________________

11 ____________________

Write a definition for each of the underlined *idioms*.

12 James felt <u>over the moon</u> when he won the trophy.

____

13 Meena was feeling <u>under the weather</u> having eaten five bags of crisps.

____

14 Ben had <u>a change of heart</u>; he didn't want to play outside in the rain!

____

Write a definition for each of these words.

15 ponder ______________________

16 unmistakable ______________________

17 cooperate ______________________

18 occupation ______________________

19 percentage ______________________

20 submerge ______________________

Circle the *diminutives*.

21–25 duckling calf piglet

eaglet bullock fawn

lamb owlet foal

Complete each sentence as a *simile*.

26 Aimee's bed was as warm as ______________________.

27 Jacob ran as fast as ______________________.

28 The custard was as thick as ______________________.

29 Jess felt as cold as ______________________.

30 Tom's bruise was as big as ______________________.

Total

Test 6: **Mixed**

Test time: 0 5 10 minutes

Circle the silent letter in each of these words.

1 guilt

2 knuckle

3 rhombus

4 island

5 gnat

6 crescent

7 crumb

8 answer

What are the following: commands, questions or statements?

9 Put your homework on the table ________________

10 What time is our appointment ________________

11 Global warming is a serious problem ________________

12 It's six o'clock ________________

13 Where have I put my recorder ________________

14 Sit quietly ________________

Add the missing apostrophes.

15–16 Ill run and get my coat from Henrys house.

17 Wheres my hat?

18 Isnt it time the cinema doors opened?

Write four words used in English but derived from another language.
Example: croissant

19 ____________________

20 ____________________

21 ____________________

22 ____________________

What parts of speech are each of these words?

23 after ________________

24 scream ________________

25 he ________________

26 tarantula ________________

27 frantically ________________

Write three sentences, each using the given phrases.

28 as a consequence

____

29 on the other hand

____

30 in contrast to

____

Total

Test 7: Grammar

Test time: 0 5 10 minutes

Write two examples of each of the following.

1–2 common nouns __________________ __________________

3–4 abstract nouns __________________ __________________

5–6 proper nouns __________________ __________________

7–8 collective nouns __________________ __________________

Fill each gap with an *adverb*.

9 Matthew looked __________________ at the sweets.

10 Hannah copied her story __________________.

11 The Gallop family __________________ waved goodbye to their cousins.

12 Jacob __________________ tidied his messy room.

Write two *adjectives* to describe each of these nouns.

13–14 ________________ , ________________ hair

15–16 a ______________ , ________________ lion

17–18 a ______________ , ________________ butterfly

Write two sentences that begin with *fronted adverbials*.

19 ____

20 ____

Underline the *preposition* in each sentence.

21 Shall we meet after breakfast?

22 Jessica's cat slept on her bed.

23 Let's see how far we can swim under the water.

24 Carl jumped over the broken gate.

Write three sentences, each with a *comparative adjective* and a *conjunction*.

25–26 ____

27–28 ____

29–30 ____

Total

Test time: 0 5 10 minutes

Read this poem carefully.

The Sands of Dee

"O Mary, go and call the cattle home,
And call the cattle home,
And call the cattle home,
Across the sands of Dee;"
The western wind was wild and dank with foam,
And all alone went she.

The western tide crept up along the sand,
And o'er and o'er the sand,
And round and round the sand,
As far as eye could see.
The rolling mist came down and hid the land:
And never home came she.

"Oh, is it weed, or fish, or floating hair –
A tress of golden hair,
A drowned maiden's hair
Above the nets at sea?
Was never salmon yet that shone so fair
Among the stakes on Dee."

They rowed her in across the rolling foam,
The cruel, crawling foam,
The cruel, hungry foam,
To her grave beside the sea:
But still the boatmen hear her call the cattle home,
Across the sands of Dee.

by Charles Kingsley

Answer these questions about the poem.

1 What was Mary asked to do?

2 When Mary set off, what was the weather like?

3 'The rolling mist came down and hid the land:'
What image does this line conjure up in your mind?

4 Copy the line in the poem that informs us of Mary's death.

5 Why do you think the sea foam is described as cruel?

6 Where was Mary buried?

7 Which word in the poem means damp or moist?

8 What does 'o'er' mean?

9 How do you think Mary felt when she was sent out to the sands of Dee?

10 Describe how this poem makes you feel.

Time for a break! Go to Puzzle Page 43

Total

Test 9: **Mixed**

Test time: 0 5 10 minutes

Underline the correct verb form in each sentence.

1 When (is/are) we going to get to Gran's house?

2 (Is/Are) we meeting this afternoon?

3 Todd's parents (was/were) pleased with his progress.

4 It (was/were) raining outside.

5 Which pony (is/are) Jodie's?

Add *tious* or *cious* to complete each word.

6 suspi ____________________

7 infec ____________________

8 ambi ____________________

9 vi ____________________

10 nutri ____________________

Write each of these words correctly.

11 embarras ____________________

12 seperate ____________________

13 marvelous ____________________

14 vegtable ____________________

15 resturant ____________________

Write a short conversation between two friends discussing what they might do after school. Be careful to start new lines when they are needed and to punctuate the conversation correctly.

16–25

Write five *synonyms* for the word 'nice'.

26

27

28

29

30

Total

Test 10: **Sentences**

Test time: 0 5 10 minutes

Write these statements as questions.

1 The water is too deep to swim in.

____

2 Andy is hiding in the woods.

____

3 Bola isn't allowed out on his bike.

____

4 My birthday is in February.

____

5 It takes Sophie thirty minutes to walk to school.

____

Write two sentences. Each sentence needs to have two commas.

6–7 ______________________________

____

8–9 ______________________________

____

Rewrite this short passage correctly. Remember to begin a new line when a different person starts to speak.

10–20 Is it Gym Club tonight asked Thomas It always is on Monday replied Poppy Thomas groaned he'd forgotten his PE kit again

____

____

____

Rewrite these sentences without double negatives.

21 We didn't want no homework.

____

22 Jake hasn't no problem learning his spellings.

____

23 Dad couldn't find no gap in which to park his car.

____

Write two sentences that indicate parenthesis using commas, brackets or dashes.

24 ______________________________

25 ______________________________

Total

Test 11: **Mixed**

Test time: 0 5 10 minutes

Draw lines to link each old word with the modern word.

1	saith	are
2	remaineth	here
3	hither	says
4	abides	remain
5	art	lives

Complete each sentence with a *phrase* or *clause*.

6 Miss James ____

____ waited for the class to listen.

7 The cat ____

____ pounced on its prey.

8 Todd's computer ____

____ frequently broke down.

9 The policeman ____

____ kept an eye on the man.

10 The sun ____

____ melted the ice cream in minutes.

Write two words, at least one hyphenated, using each of these prefixes.

11–12 bi ________________ ________________

13–14 non ________________ ________________

15–16 cross ________________ ________________

17–18 co ________________ ________________

19–20 re ________________ ________________

Fill each gap with an *adjective* and noun.

21 Sam screamed and ran from the ________________________________.

22 Jack snuggled closely to the ________________________________.

23 Freda rushed towards the ________________________________.

24 Joseph raced after the ________________________________.

Add 'able' or 'ible' to complete each word.

25 charge________

26 irresist________

27 convert________

28 extend________

29 regrett________

30 avoid________

Total

Test 12: **Spelling**

Test time: 0 5 10 minutes

List five *ough* words. Each word must illustrate a different pronunciation of the *ough* letter pattern.

1–5 ____________________

____

____

____

____

Write each of these words correctly.

6 imediately ____________________

7 relevent ____________________

8 secratary ____________________

9 temprature ____________________

10 excellant ____________________

Add ance or ence to each of these to make a word.

11 appear________

12 eleg________

13 radi________

14 occurr________

15 sil________

16 experi________

Add ant or ent to each of these to make a word.

17 pleas________

18 hesit________

19 magnific________

20 abund________

21 stagn________

22 transpar________

Answers

Answers will vary for questions that require children to answer in their own words. Possible answers to most of these questions are given in *italics*.

Test 1: Mixed

1 The leaf fell from the tree.
2 The child played with a skipping rope and a football.
3 While playing, the kitten knocked the bag to the floor.
4 The swing broke and injured a child.
5 to divide
6 to state
7 to infect
8 to detect
9 unhappy
10 defrost
11 ungrateful
12 incorrect
13 unclean
14 disadvantage
15 Too many cooks spoil the broth.
16 The grass is always greener on the other side.
17 While the cat's away the mice will play.
18 Every cloud has a silver lining.
19 The early bird catches the worm.
20 their
21–22 their, they're
23 There
24 busily
25 argument
26 laughing
27 noticeable
28 completely
29 imaginary
30 meaningless

Test 2: Spelling

1 unnecessary
2 desperate
3 recommend
4 appreciate
5 harass
6 determined
7 bargain
8 environment
9 interrupt
10 curiosity
11 *misbehave*
12 *recharge*
13 *tricycle*
14 *automobile*
15 *unready*
16 *misfortune*
17–18 *special official*
19–20 *partial substantial*
21 churches
22 waltzes
23 bushes
24 pencils
25 wives
26 brief
27 sleigh
28 eighty
29 fierce
30 feint
31 siege
32 reign
33 ceiling
34 **k**nockout
35 colum**n**
36 mini**a**ture
37 **p**salm
38 **g**nat
39 clim**b**er
40 **g**nome

Test 3: Comprehension

1 Young wood-lice are controlled by their elders.
2 *Wood-lice elders are strict and set in their ways.*
3 Wood-lice whiskers have to be 3 millimetres long.
4 *The parents of the young wood-lice would have felt proud that their young were attending the meeting but also probably a little nervous.*
5 The purpose of the meeting is to remind themselves of the purpose of life.
6 He was often in trouble for asking too many questions.
7 *brought together*
8 *he moved with displeasure*
9 *The wood-lice were shocked because nobody ever asked the Chief Wood-louse questions.*
10 *Child's own answer*

Test 4: Mixed

1 *sunlight*
2 *handbag*
3 *snowball*
4 *penknife*
5 *lighthouse*
6 *trapdoor*
7 *football*
8 *rainfall*
9 *Zoe shouted that if we didn't hurry we'd be late.*
10 *Beth enquired whether that was the way to the toilets.*
11 *Dan screamed that we had to be quick as the guard dog was catching us.*
12 *Mrs Sparks asked what time it was.*
13 *Mum whispered to remind me that when I woke up in the morning it would be my birthday.*
14 serial
15 grate
16 hoarse
17 bow
18 beech
19 herd
20 weight
21 peace
22 scent or cent
23–40 Class 6 was having a swimming lesson.
"I'm exhausted," exclaimed Eva. "I wish something more exciting would happen."
"I agree because if I do one more length of this pool I'll scream!" moaned Lee.
Suddenly, Eva's wish came true as Mrs Davey, their teacher, slipped on some water at the side of the pool. She fell headfirst into the pool!

Test 5: Vocabulary

1 *ask for*
2 *unhappiness*
3 *unable to avoid*
4 *find out*
5 *go in*
6–11 *cried, exclaimed, laughed, replied, shouted, thought.*
12 *very pleased*
13 *sick*
14 *changed his mind*
15 *to think carefully about something*
16 *clear, obvious*
17 *to work willingly with others*
18 *a job or something to fill one's time*
19 *something divided into a hundred parts*
20 *to go under water*
21–25 duckling, piglet, eaglet, bullock, owlet
26 *toast*
27 *a cheetah*
28 *cement*
29 *ice*
30 *an apple*

Test 6: Mixed

1 u
2 k
3 h
4 s
5 g
6 c
7 b
8 w
9 command
10 question
11 statement
12 statement
13 question
14 command
15–16 I'll run and ... Henry's house.
17 Where's my hat?
18 Isn't it time the ...
19–22 *pizza, origami, umbrella, siesta.*
23 preposition or conjunction
24 verb or noun
25 pronoun
26 noun
27 adverb
28–30 Child to include the three given phrases into their own sentences.

Test 7: Grammar

1–2 *chair, house*
3–4 *love, beauty*
5–6 *Beth, England*
7–8 *crowd, gaggle*
9 *longingly*
10 *neatly*
11 *sadly*
12 *grumpily*
13–14 *long, black*
15–16 *large, snarling*
17–18 *small, fragile*
19–20 Two sentences beginning with fronted adverbials, e.g. *Before we leave, go to the toilet*
21 after
22 on
23 under
24 over
25–30 *Child's own answer*

Test 8: Comprehension

1 *Mary was asked to call the cattle home.*
2 *There was a wild wind when Mary set off.*
3 *Child's own answer*
4 'A drowned maiden's hair'
5 *The sea is described as cruel, as it was the sea in which Mary died.*
6 *Mary was buried beside the sea.*
7 dank
8 over
9 *Child's own answer*
10 *Child's own answer*

Test 9: Mixed

1 are
2 Are
3 were
4 was
5 is
6 suspicious
7 infectious
8 ambitious
9 vicious
10 nutritious
11 embarrass
12 separate
13 marvellous
14 vegetable
15 restaurant
16–25 *Child's own answer. Give marks for correct layout and punctuation.*
26–30 *pleasant, lovely, enjoyable, good, likeable.*

Test 10: Sentences

1 Is the water too deep to swim in?
2 Is Andy hiding in the woods?
3 Isn't Bola allowed out on his bike?
4 Is my birthday in February?
5 Does it take Sophie thirty minutes to walk to school?
6–9 *Child's own answer*
10–20 "Is it Gym Club tonight**?**" asked Thomas**.**
"It always is on Monday**,**" replied Poppy**.**
Thomas groaned**.** He**'**d forgotten his PE kit again**.**
21 We didn't want any homework.
22 Jake hasn't a problem learning his spellings. *or* Jake has no problem learning his spellings.
23 Dad couldn't find a gap in which to park his car. *or* Dad could find no gap in which to park his car.
24–25 Two sentences illustrating the use of brackets, dashes or commas in parenthesis, e.g. *Jess and her friends (Aman and Janice) caught the bus to town.*

Test 11: Mixed

1 saith – says
2 remaineth – remain
3 hither – here
4 abides – lives
5 art – are
6–10 *Child's own answer*
11–12 *bi-monthly, bicycle*
13–14 *non-smoker, nonsense*
15–16 *cross-section, crossroad*
17–18 *co-operate, coexist*
19–20 *re-cover, rewrite*
21 *haunted house*
22 *crackling fire*
23 *shoe shop*
24 *small dog*
25 chargeable
26 irresistible
27 convertible
28 extendable
29 regrettable
30 avoidable

Test 12: Spelling

1–5 *bought, borough, enough, through, bough*
6 immediately
7 relevant
8 secretary
9 temperature
10 excellent
11 appearance
12 elegance
13 radiance
14 occurrence
15 silence
16 experience
17 pleasant
18 hesitant
19 magnificent
20 abundant
21 stagnant
22 transparent
23 garden
24 ornament
25 resist
26 notice

27 shine
28 happy
29 alter
30 giraffe
31 pulley
32 grammar
33 professor
34 necessary
35 wrapping
36 preferring
37 referral
38 preference
39 transferred
40 referring

Test 13: Comprehension

1 Pedigree dogs are the most expensive to buy.
2 Some pedigree dogs are unsuitable to keep as pets because they are traditionally bred to work.
3 A Dalmatian needs plenty of exercise.
4 It is possible to estimate the size of a cross-bred dog when both parents are known.
5 *Cross-breds are cheaper to buy, stronger in constitution and less highly strung.*
6 A mongrel dog's parents are of mixed ancestry; a mix of different dogs.
7 Some mongrels are difficult to home because it is hard to predict accurately how they will develop since their sires are unknown.
8 *Child's own answer*
9 offspring
10 sturdy

Test 14: Mixed

1 bushes
2 athletes
3 convoys
4 motifs
5 kangaroos
6 babies
7–9 *Child's own answers, e.g.* ***U****sing* ***n****ew* ***n****apkins* ***e****ight* ***c****hildren* ***e****at* ***s****ugary* ***s****weets* ***a****nd* ***r****aspberry* ***y****oghurts.*
10–11 Grandad**,** who was feeling grumpy anyway**,** got really cross ...
12–13 ... perhaps the sound of the wind howling**,** sirens screaming**,** leaves rustling ...
14 To be able to understand your own beliefs and values**,** you need to ...
15–16 *friendly, friendship*
17–18 *shameful, shameless*
19–20 *happiness, happily*
21–22 *painful, painless*
23–24 *greatness, greatly*
25–30 *Child's sentences illustrating colons and semicolons, e.g.*
We have two types of tree in our garden: beech and oak.
It's snowing; I'm so excited.
People enjoy summer for a number of reasons: it's warm; they enjoy doing things outside; they can eat BBQs; it stays light late into the evening.

Test 15: Vocabulary

1–5 *Child's own sentences. Five sentences containing the listed words.*
6 husband
7 prince
8 nephew
9 gentleman
10 lion
11 fox
12–15 television, DVD player, astronaut, website
16 compact disc
17 kilogram
18 United States of America
19 South East or Stock Exchange
20 Member of Parliament
21–22 *outfit, outlaw*
23–24 *thrill, throne*
25–26 *disgrace, dispatch*
27 *The wind was a howling beast.*
28 *The snow is soft balls of cotton wool.*
29 *The leaves are a prickly carpet.*
30 *His bedroom was a tip!*

Test 16: Mixed

1–8 common noun: *man*
proper noun: *Lucy*
abstract noun: *appearance*
collective noun: *bunch*
9 "Ben, it is time to put the chips in the oven," called Mum.
10 "There's nothing to worry about," said the vet.
11 "It's time for lunch," announced Mrs Owen.
12 "Rupesh, would you like to stay the night at my house?" asked Ryan.
13–17 *Child's own sentences using the words or phrases listed correctly.*
18 *The water was as blue as sapphire.*
19 *The swan was as white as snow.*
20 *The drum was as loud as a thunder clap.*
21 *Jo saw a spider that was as big as a house.*
22 *The monkey sat as quiet as a mouse.*
23 marine
24 claim
25 post
26 digest
27 rely
28 nation
29 hygiene
30 offence

Test 17: Grammar

1–2 *ran quickly*
3–4 *worked slowly*
5–6 *searched helplessly*
7–8 *sat patiently*
9–10 *talked quietly*
11–15 *child's own answer*
16 *an unusually large banana*
17 *the extremely naughty children*
18 *a scary black spider*
19 *the suprisingly calm wind*
20 *a really exciting computer game*
21–22 *friendship, hatred*
23–24 *above, under*
25–26 *(to) sit, (to) laugh*
27–28 *it, he*
29–30 *the smallest, the largest*

Test 18: Comprehension

1 The Second World War.
2 He let him win at marbles; he lent him his wicket keeper's gloves; he gave him his best stamp.

3 Everyone knew when he arrived at school with grazed knees, dirt on his blazer and red eyes from crying.
4 He believed this because the boy's father was an electrician rather than being at the front line.
5 *Child's own answer*
6 He worked in a button factory.
7 *Child's own answer*
8 *He was hiding his embarrassment about the fact that his father hadn't gone off to fight in the war.*
9 *Child's own answer*
10 Most men were going off to fight in the war, and those who died were thought of as heroes.

Test 19: Mixed

1 *Two people can be more successful at doing something than one person.*
2 *You get better at something with practice.*
3 *If you help me, I will help you.*
4 *It is best not to change things.*
5–11 **"**Can I open my present now**?"** asked Gina**. "**I have waited a very long time**!"**
12–16 "Let's go ice-skating," suggested Jenny.
17–18 *crash, whoosh*
19–20 *hissing, slithering*
21–22 *whizz, fizzle*
23 pronoun
24 conjunction
25 adverb
26 verb or noun
27 verb or noun
28–30 *Child's own answers*

Test 20: Sentences

1 were
2 was
3 were
4 was
5 was
6–8 *Child's own answers*
9–10 Two sentences that include a relative clause, e.g. *That's the girl who lives near my friend.*
11–15 **"Q**uieten down**!"** bellowed the headteacher**.**
16–18 **D**arren raced towards the ball**,** not wanting to be beaten by anyone**.**
19–23 **"A**re we going to win**?"** called Helen**.**
24–26 Three passive sentences, e.g. *The dog was being walked by the boy.*
27 **D**ave's cats, **B**atman and **R**obin, tore up his **H**arry **P**otter poster.
28 **T**he train was late, eventually arriving in **M**anchester after **M**anchester **U**nited had won their match!

Puzzle 1

1 South Africa
2 department store
3 Downing Street
4 pencil crayon
5 shopping trolley
6 Prince William
7 swimming costume
8 Blue Peter
A and B *Child's own answers*

Puzzle 2

necessary, innocent, receive, decision

gaol, religion, vegetable, imagination

Puzzle 3

For example:

happy – happily, happiest, unhappy

phone – telephone, microphone, phoneme

question – questioning, questionable, questioned

detect – detective, detecting, detectable

graph – telegraph, autograph, photograph

Puzzle 4

Child's own answers

Puzzle 5

Across	Down
2 bicycle	**1** octagon
3 triathlon	**4** tripod
5 octopus	
6 decade	

Write the *root word* of each of these words.

23 gardener ____________________

24 ornamental ____________________

25 resistance ____________________

26 noticeable ____________________

27 shiny ____________________

28 happiness ____________________

29 alteration ____________________

Add the missing double letters to each of these words.

30 gira__ __e

31 pu__ __ey

32 gra__ __ar

33 profe__ __or

34 nece__ __ary

35 wra__ __ing

Complete these word sums. Watch out for the spelling changes!

36 prefer + ing = ____________________

37 refer + al = ____________________

38 prefer + ence = ____________________

39 transfer + ed = ____________________

40 refer + ing = ____________________

Time for a break! Go to Puzzle Page 44

Total

Test time: 0 5 10 minutes

Read this extract carefully.

Pedigree or mongrel?

Pedigree dogs

Pedigree, or pure-bred, dogs are the most expensive to buy, but it is not usually difficult to find homes for their puppies. Being highly bred may make them more delicate than dogs of mixed ancestry and more likely to inherit defects. The very fact that they are descended from a line of dogs used traditionally for a particular form of work may make some of them unsuitable as pets for the average household. Dalmatians, for instance, were once carriage dogs. A pair of them would run alongside the horses in the capacity of outriders. Their elegant proportions and attractive, spotted coats mean they are now in demand as pets, but they should only be kept if they can be allowed plenty of exercise.

Cross-bred dogs

Cross-breds are the **progeny** of two pure-bred parents of different breeds. Cross-breds usually make very good pets. They are cheaper to buy, but of course cost as much to keep as pedigree dogs. When both parents are known, it is possible to estimate the adult size and type of cross-bred puppy. Depending on the combination of the parents' characteristics, a cross-bred dog can be very attractive, and may be stronger in constitution and often less highly strung than either of its parents.

Mongrel dogs

Mongrels are dogs of mixed ancestry. They are inexpensive and most make affectionate companions. Nearly all mongrels are **robust**, but since their sires are often unknown, it is impossible to predict accurately how mongrel puppies will develop. This is one reason why mongrels are difficult to home, and why so many are taken to animal welfare societies, such as the RSPCA, from which they can sometimes be adopted.

The Official RSPCA Pet Guide

Care for Your Dog

Answer these questions about the extract.

1 Which type of dog is most expensive to buy?

2 Why are some pedigree dogs unsuitable to keep as pets for the average household?

3 If a Dalmatian is kept as a pet what does it particularly need?

4 When is it possible to estimate the adult size of a cross-bred dog?

5 Write three differences between pedigree and cross-bred dogs.

6 Describe the parents of a mongrel dog.

7 Why are some mongrel dogs difficult to home?

8 Which type of dog would you choose to keep and why?

9 What is meant by the word **'progeny'**?

10 What does **'robust'** mean?

Total

Test 14: **Mixed**

Test time: 0 5 10 minutes

Write each of these nouns in its plural form.

1 bush ________________

2 athlete ________________

3 convoy ________________

4 motif ________________

5 kangaroo ________________

6 baby ________________

Write a *mnemonic* to help you remember how to spell each of these words.

7 accommodate

____

8 government

____

9 unnecessary

____

Add the missing commas to these sentences.

10–11 Grandad who was feeling grumpy anyway got really cross when the puppy chewed his new slippers.

12–13 Take a few moments to listen to different sounds – perhaps the sound of the wind howling sirens screaming leaves rustling or buzzing planes.

14 To be able to understand your own beliefs and values you need to learn about the beliefs and values of others.

Add two suffixes to each of these to make new words.

15–16 friend ______ ______

17–18 shame ______ ______

19–20 happy ______ ______

21–22 pain ______ ______

23–24 great ______ ______

Write three sentences, one with a colon, one with a semicolon and one with a colon introducing a list using three semicolons.

25 ______

26 ______

27–30 ______

______

______

______

Total

Test 15: **Vocabulary**

Test time: 0 5 10 minutes

Write each of these words in a sentence.

withhold

1 ______________________________

access

2 ______________________________

opportunity

3 ______________________________

persistence

4 ______________________________

mischievous

5 ______________________________

Write the masculine gender of each of these words.

6	wife	____________	**9**	lady	____________
7	princess	____________	**10**	lioness	____________
8	niece	____________	**11**	vixen	____________

Circle the words that have come into our language in the last 100 years.

12–15

chimney television box

pottery DVD player glass astronaut

bicycle website mantelpiece

Write these *abbreviations* in full.

16 CD ____________________

17 kg ____________________

18 USA ____________________

19 SE ____________________

20 MP ____________________

Fill the gaps with two words. The four words in each set need to be in alphabetical order.

21–22 outback ________ ________ outsider

23–24 thread ________ ________ thrush

25–26 disease ________ ________ distress

Write a *metaphor* for each of these subjects.

27 wind

____

28 snow

____

29 leaves

____

30 bedroom

____

Total

TEST 16: **Mixed**

Test time: 0 5 10 minutes

List the four different types of noun. Write an example of each.

1–2 ____________ noun Example: ____________

3–4 ____________ noun Example: ____________

5–6 ____________ noun Example: ____________

7–8 ____________ noun Example: ____________

Write these sentences as *direct speech*.

9 Mum called to Ben that it was time to put the chips in the oven.

____

10 The vet told me there was nothing to worry about.

____

11 Mrs Owen announced it was time for lunch.

____

12 Ryan asked Rupesh if he would like to stay the night at his house.

____

____

Write five sentences. In each sentence use the listed word or phrase correctly.

13 man eating shark ____________

14 hot-water bottle ____________

15 recover ____________

16 small-business manager ____________

17 heavy metal detector ____________

Write a *simile* using the following subjects.

18 water

____

19 swan

____

20 drum

____

21 spider

____

22 monkey

____

Write the *root word* of each of these words.

23 submarine ______________

24 exclaim ______________

25 postage ______________

26 digestible ______________

27 reliable ______________

28 international ______________

29 hygienic ______________

30 offensive ______________

Time for a break! Go to Puzzle Page 45

Total

TEST 17: Grammar

Test time: 0 5 10 minutes

Add a different verb and *adverb* to each sentence.

1–2 Fiona ______________ ______________ to the other side of the playground.

3–4 The postman ______________ ______________ in the rain.

5–6 The abandoned dog ______________ ______________ for his home.

7–8 The bird ______________ ______________ on her eggs waiting for them to hatch.

9–10 Mrs Seal's class ______________ ______________ as they waited for lunch.

Complete these sentences. Use a *conjunction* from the box in each one. You may use each word only once.

because	but	if	when	and

11 Molly loved her party dress ____

____

12 Reuben had saved his pocket money for weeks ________________________

____

13 Bill and Jake planned to meet in town ______________________________

____

14 The snake watched the mouse ____________________________________

____

15 The sheep escaped from their field ________________________________

____

Write an *adjectival phrase* about each of these nouns.

16 a banana

____

17 the children

____

18 a spider

____

19 the wind

____

20 a computer game

____

Write two examples of each of the following.

21–22	abstract noun	________	________
23–24	preposition	________	________
25–26	verb	________	________
27–28	pronoun	________	________
29–30	superlative adjective	________	________

Total

Test time: 0 5 10 minutes

Read this extract carefully.

Hurricane Summer *by Robert Swindells*

Funny things, friendships. They tend to come and go, but most people have a special friend who stands out among all the others. I'm lucky – I've got two. One of them's been dead a long time now, but it doesn't matter – he'll always be my friend. As for the other ... well, as I said, friendships are funny. Best thing I can do is tell you about them.

The Second World War was on and I was ten. I was an only child. My dad had been killed the previous autumn serving with the Navy. Mum said I must always remember that my dad had been a hero, and I knew he had, that was the trouble.

You see, I wasn't a hero. Far from it.

There was this lad at school. Clive Simcox. He was the same age as me – we were in the same class – but Clive was taller and heavier, and for some reason that summer he started picking on me. I didn't like fighting so I was forever trying to please him. I let him win at marbles and lent him my wicket keeper's gloves. I even gave him my best stamp – a Guadeloupe triangular – but it was no use. He'd still ambush me on the way home from school and bash me up. He used to wait for me in the mornings too, and trip me as I ran past. I'd arrive at school with grazed knees and dirt on my blazer and red eyes from crying, and everybody would know Clive had had another go at me.

He used to make remarks about my Dad, which was even worse. Before the war Dad had been an electrician, so they made him an electrician in the Navy. I don't know what his work was exactly, but it had to do with electrical circuits and that sort of thing. Anyway, Clive had latched on to this and sometimes he'd say, "He **was nothing special**, you know, your dad. He wasn't a gunner or a torpedo man. He didn't kill any Germans. He was just an electrician, mending fuses and changing lightbulbs while other fellows did the fighting." This would be in the playground or on the street and he'd say it at the top of his voice so everyone could hear, and all the time he'd be pushing me – shoving me in the chest so that I had to keep stepping backwards. He was goading me of course – trying to make me fight, but I was too scared. Red-faced with shame, I'd retreat till he got bored and went off to bother somebody else.

I **despised** myself. I'd think, what sort of kid doesn't stick up for his dead father? Defend his honour? If I was half the hero Dad was, I'd stand up to Simcox and punch him on the nose, even if he bashed me up after ... When it came to it – when he was actually there in front of me with his red face and mocking eyes – I'd either try to run or let him hit me to get it over. I was ashamed of myself but I couldn't help it.

Funniest thing was, Simcox senior wasn't even in the forces. He worked in a button factory, but I daren't bring that up when Clive was tormenting me. Shows how scared I was, and believe me it's no joke being a coward when the world seems **full of heroes**.

Answer these questions about the extract.

1. In which war had the boy's father died? ______________________

2. List the three ways the boy tried to please Clive Simcox.

____

____

3. How did everyone know when Clive had bullied the boy?

____

4. Why did Clive Simcox believe the boy's father **'was nothing special'**?

____

5. In your own words describe why the boy **'despised'** himself.

____

6. What did Clive Simcox's dad do during the war?

____

7. How do you think Clive Simcox felt while bullying the boy?

____

____

8. Why do you think Clive Simcox was a bully?

____

____

9. When you see someone being bullied how do you feel?

____

____

10. Why did the world seem **'full of heroes'**?

____

____

Total

TEST 19: Mixed

Test time: 0 5 10 minutes

Write the meaning of each of these proverbs.

1 Two heads are better than one.

2 Practice makes perfect.

3 You scratch my back and I'll scratch yours.

4 Let sleeping dogs lie.

Rewrite these sentences with the missing punctuation.

5–11 Can I open my present now asked Gina I have waited a very long time

12–16 Lets go ice-skating suggested Jenny

Write two *onomatopoeic* words that can describe each of these.

17–18 an avalanche ____________ ____________

19–20 a snake ____________ ____________

21–22 a firework ____________ ____________

What parts of speech are each of these words?

23 it ____________

24 but ____________

25 grumpily ____________

26 hate ____________

27 remove ____________

Write an example of each of the following.

28 a question

____

29 a statement

____

30 a command

____

Total

Test 20: **Sentences**

Test time: 0 5 10 minutes

Add 'was' or 'were' to each sentence to make it correct.

1 The Jacob family __________ relieved to reach their holiday home.

2 The dog barked excitedly every time the ball __________ thrown to him.

3 Mrs Trevis's children __________ very well-behaved during the concert.

4 Half the audience cheered when the villain __________ caught.

5 Hannah __________ too excited to sleep.

Complete each sentence with a *phrase* or *clause*.

6 The horses ______________________________

______________________________ waited for their morning feed.

7 Ben rode his bike ______________________________

______________________________ to Tuhil's house.

8 Rebecca ______________________________

______________________________ waited for her brother.

Write two sentences that include a *relative clause*.

9 ______________________________

10 ______________________________

Rewrite these sentences correctly.

11–15 quieten down bellowed the headteacher

____

16–18 darren raced towards the ball not wanting to be beaten by anyone

____

____

19–23 are we going to win called Helen

____

____

Write three sentences using the passive voice. Remember, a sentence is written in the passive voice when the subject of the sentence has an action done to it by someone or something else.

24 ______________________________

25 ______________________________

26 ______________________________

Circle the letters in these sentences that need capitals.

27 dave's cats, batman and robin, tore up his harry potter poster.

28 the train was late, eventually arriving in manchester after manchester united had won their match!

Time for a break! Go to Puzzle Page 46

Total

Puzzle 1

In each of these groups of letters there are two words muddled together but with the letters placed in the correct order.

Can you sort the muddled words?

All capital letters are missing. Use the clues to help.

1 asfroiutcha
(a country) ____________ ____________

2 sdtepoarrtmenet
(a type of shop) ____________ ____________

3 dsotwrneientg
(a place in London) ____________ ____________

4 crpeanciylon
(can be used to mark paper) ____________ ____________

5 strhooppllienyg
(used in a supermarket) ____________ ____________

6 wprirlnlicame
(a famous person) ____________ ____________

7 csoswitmumimnge
(needed when doing the crawl or breaststroke) ____________ ____________

8 bpeltueer
(a television programme) ____________ ____________

Write some muddled words and clues of your own.

Try them out on someone.

A ____

____

B ____

____

Puzzle 2

Find four soft c and four soft g words in this wordsearch.

b	k	r	e	c	e	i	v	e	v
n	d	g	n	s	t	m	d	f	e
e	g	a	o	l	f	a	c	n	g
c	x	k	c	a	k	g	o	g	e
e	r	e	l	i	g	i	o	n	t
s	a	d	b	t	s	n	b	s	a
s	f	d	n	i	d	a	d	n	b
a	n	s	c	b	s	t	n	t	l
r	c	e	t	o	z	i	m	b	e
y	d	o	g	n	d	o	c	g	a
i	n	n	o	c	e	n	t	o	k

Write the words you have found.

soft c words	soft g words
__________	__________
__________	__________
__________	__________
__________	__________

Puzzle 3

How many words can you find from the same word family?

spark

sparkler

sparkling

sparkle

happy

phone

question

detect

graph

Puzzle 4

As time passes more and more words are being invented.

For example the word 'cheeseburger' was invented to describe a hamburger that had cheese added to it.

Invent your own words for:

a hovering skateboard ________________________

a jam and ham sandwich ________________________

someone who always walks backwards ________________________

an animal that speaks ________________________

someone who can fly ________________________

a pot plant that asks for water when it needs it ________________________

Invent three more words with your own definitions.

____

____

____

Puzzle 5

Complete the crossword.

Each of the answers begins with a number prefix.
The clues will help you!

Across

2 A two-wheeled vehicle.

3 A race in three parts.

5 An underwater animal with eight tentacles.

6 Ten years.

Down

1 A shape with eight sides.

4 A stand often used with a camera.

Key words

Some special words are used in this book. You will find them picked out in *italics*. These words are explained here.

abbreviation	a word that has been shortened
abstract noun	a noun referring to a concept or idea, e.g. love, beauty
adjectival phrase	a group of words describing a noun
adjective	a word that describes somebody or something
adverb	a word that gives extra meaning to a verb
adverbial phrase	a word or phrase that makes the meaning of a verb, adjective or another adverb more specific, e.g. The Cheshire cat vanished *quite slowly*, beginning with the end of its tail
antonym	a word with a meaning opposite to another word, e.g. hot/cold
clause	a section of a sentence with a verb
collective noun	a noun referring to a group or collection of things, e.g. a swarm of bees
comparative	describes the amount of something (adverb or adjective), e.g. more, bigger
conjunction	a word used to link sentences, phrases or words, e.g. and, but
contraction	two words shortened into one with an apostrophe placed where the letter/s have been dropped, e.g. do not/don't
diminutive	a word implying smallness, e.g. duckling
fronted adverbial	an adverbial that has been moved before the verb, e.g. *The day after tomorrow*, I'm going on holiday
homophone	a word that has the same sound as another but a different meaning or spelling, e.g. right/write
idiom	a phrase that is not meant literally
infinitive	the basic form of the verb, e.g. to scream
metaphor	a figurative expression in which something is described in terms usually associated with something else, e.g. the sky is a sapphire sea
mnemonic	a way of aiding the memory, e.g. a rhyme or silly story
modal verb	verbs that change the meaning of other verbs, e.g. can, will
onomatopoeic	a word that echoes a sound, associated with its meaning, e.g. hiss
parenthesis	this is a word or phrase that is separated off from the main sentence by brackets, commas or dashes usually because it contains additional information not essential to its understanding
phrase	a group of words that do not contain both a subject and a verb
preposition	a word that links nouns and pronouns to other parts of a sentence, e.g. he sat *behind* the door
pronoun	a word that can be used instead of a noun
relative clause	a special type of subordinate clause that makes the meaning of a noun more specific, e.g. The prize *that I won* was a book
reported speech	what has been said without using the exact words or speech marks
root word	a word to which a prefix or suffix can be added to make another word, e.g. quick – *quick*ly
simile	an expression to describe what something is like, e.g. as cold as ice
superlative	describes the limit of a quality (adjective or adverb), e.g. most, least, shortest
synonym	a word with a very similar meaning to another word, e.g. quick/fast

Progress Grid

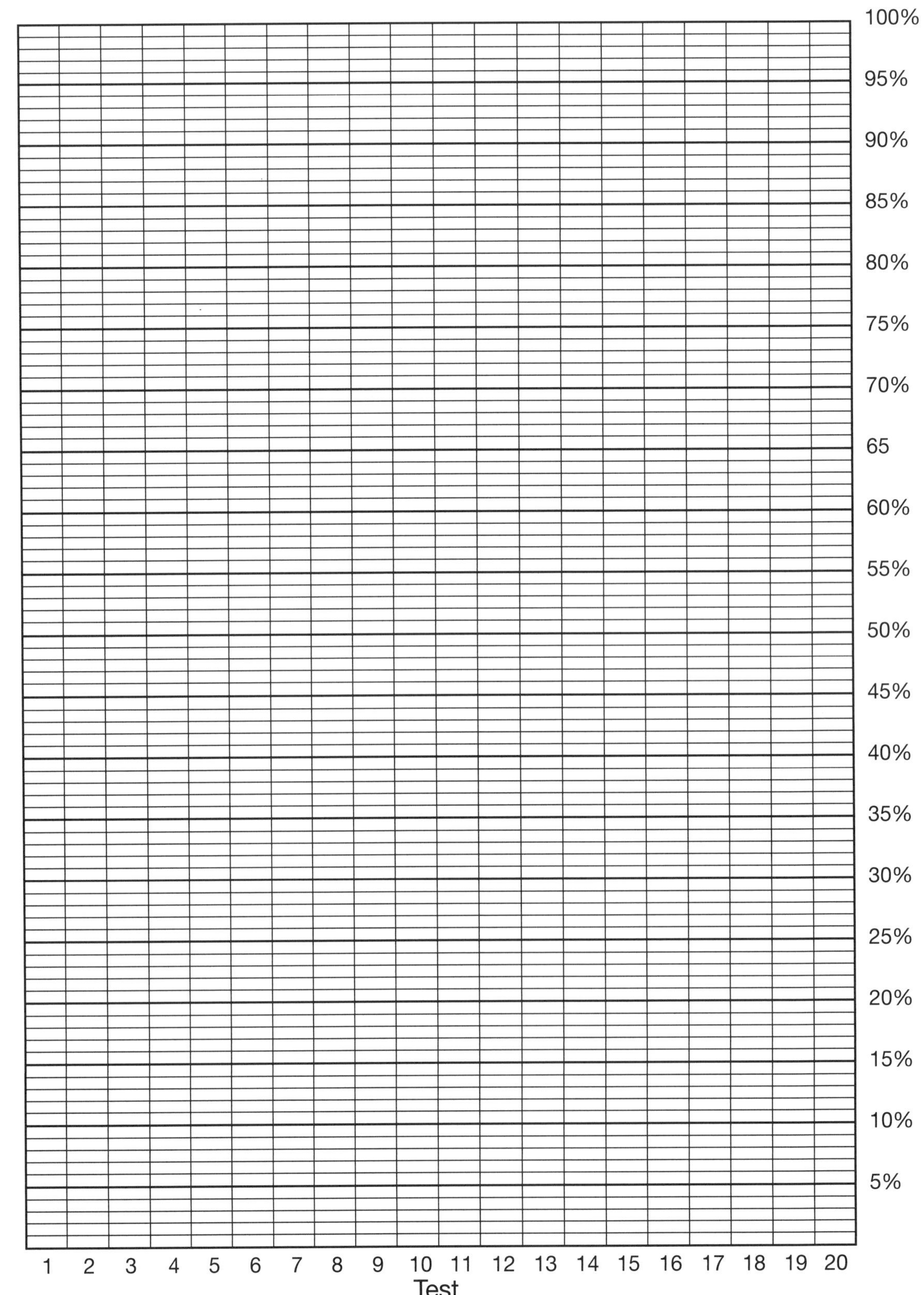